them onto the porch.

Word Bird's
Hide-and-Seek Word Bird

The Child's World

Published in the United States of America by The Child's World®, Inc.
PO Box 326
Chanhassen, MN 55317-0326
800-599-READ
www.childsworld.com

Project Manager Mary Berendes
Editor Katherine Stevenson, Ph.D.
Designer Ian Butterworth

Library of Congress Cataloging-in-Publication Data
Moncure, Jane Belk.
Hide-and-seek Word Bird / by Jane Belk Moncure.
p. cm.
Summary: Word Bird plays hide-and-seek with
his parents in their house.
ISBN 1-56766-990-5 (lib. : alk. paper)
[1. Hide-and-seek—Fiction. 2. Birds—Fiction.]   I. Title.
PZ7.M739 Hj 2002
[E]—dc21
2001006038

Word Bird's

Hide-and-Seek
Word Bird

by Jane Belk Moncure

illustrated by Chris McEwan

"Let's play hide-and-seek,"
said Word Bird.

Papa closed his eyes.
Word Bird hid.

"One, two, three. Here I come!" said Papa.

Papa looked

under the chair,

and under the rug.

Papa looked all around
the living room.

"Where are you,
Word Bird?" he asked.

"There you are...

under the couch."

"It is my turn," said Papa.
"Close your eyes,
    Word Bird."

"One, two, three. Here I
    come!" said Word Bird.

Word Bird looked behind the clock,

and behind
the door.

Word Bird looked all
around the dining room.

"Where are you, Papa?"

"There you are…

behind the cupboard."

"Let me play," said Mama.

Word Bird and Papa
closed their eyes.

Mama hid.

"One, two, three. Here
we come!" said Word
Bird and Papa.

Papa and Word Bird looked behind the stove,

and under the sink.

They looked all
around the kitchen.

"Where are you, Mama?"

"There you are...

under the table."

"Now it is time for bed," said Papa.

"Can we play one more time?" asked Word Bird.

"Just one more time,"
said Papa.

Mama and Papa closed
their eyes. Word Bird hid.

"One, two, three. Here we come!" said Mama and Papa.

Mama and Papa looked

in the closet,

and behind the dresser.

They looked all
around their bedroom.

Where are you, Word Bird?"

Then they peeked into
Word Bird's room.

Guess where Word
Bird was?

Curled up in bed, fast asleep.

Can you read these words with Word Bird?

chair

stove

rug

sink

couch

table

clock

closet

door

dresser

cupboard

bed